Don't take you~

to SCHOOL

Don't take your Elephant to SCHOOL

An alphabet of poems

Steve Turner

Illustrations by David Mostyn

LION
CHILDREN'S

Text copyright © 2006 Steve Turner
Illustrations copyright © 2006 David Mostyn
This edition copyright © 2006 Lion Hudson

The moral rights of the author and illustrator
have been asserted

A Lion Children's Book
an imprint of

Lion Hudson plc

Mayfield House, 256 Banbury Road,
Oxford OX2 7DH, England
www.lionhudson.com
ISBN-13 978 0 7459 6020 3
ISBN-10 0 7459 6020 0

First edition 2006
10 9 8 7 6 5 4 3 2 1 0

Acknowledgments

A catalogue record for this book is available
from the British Library

Typeset in 12/14 Century Schoolbook BT
Printed and bound in Great Britain by
Cox and Wyman Ltd, Reading

Introduction

Welcome to my fifth book of poetry for children! This time I've chosen the alphabet as a theme and, as usual, I set myself some challenges when I started writing it.

First, I set myself the goal of writing three poems for each letter of the alphabet. There are 26 letters in the alphabet, so can you work out how many poems are in this book?*

I wanted each title to consist of only one word, like on those wall posters that hang in classrooms where there is a picture of an apple and the letter A, a picture of a ball and the letter B, and so on. But you'll see that my titles are much more interesting!

Finally, I wanted the poems to be short. I had hoped that each poem would fit on one page and I've achieved this most of the time.

When I began writing the book I called it *Acorn Zebra* because I imagined the first poem would be about an acorn and the last about a zebra. If I had stuck to that way of thinking the book would have eventually been called *Aardvark Zoo*, but my publisher thought *Don't Take Your Elephant to School* was a much better title. (I think they're right!)

I hope that you'll enjoy reading these poems as much as I enjoyed writing them.

Steve Turner
June 2006

* There are 78 poems altogether.

To everyone whose first name begins with
QWERTYUIOPASDFGHJKLZXCVBN or M,
especially Simone Burnett of Brentwood, California,
and Matilda Taylor of Barnes, London.

Contents

A
a

Aardvark

There was a young aardvark from Kent
Whose snout was exceedingly bent.
Ants in their rows
Went up through his nose
But he never could see where they went.

Android

There was a strange baby called Neil
Who was made out of flesh-covered steel.
If he fell out of bed
Or got hit on his head
The steel under Neil couldn't feel.

Apple

An apple a day
keeps the doctor away
That's what the experts have said.
An apple a day
keeps the doctor away
Especially if thrown at his head.

Ball

Billiard balls are small and hard
Polo balls are white
Basketballs are full of bounce
Ping-pong balls are light.

Cricket balls are rosy red
Punch balls look like pears
Fairground balls are made of wood
Tennis balls have hairs.

Rugby balls are shaped like eggs
Cannon balls are fat
Bowling balls have three big holes
Punctured balls are flat.

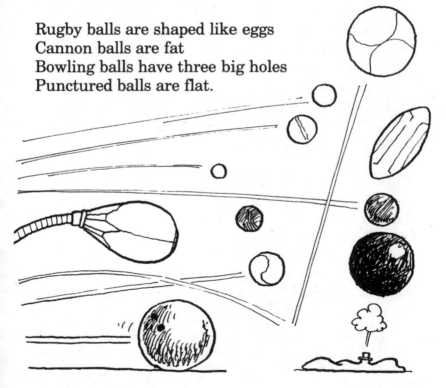

B
b

Bananas

Apples are cheerful
But frightened of heights
Pumpkins like grinning
On dark windy nights
Melons are healthy
But can put on weight
Bananas are funny
Because they're not straight.

Grapefruit are jolly
They don't have a care
Pineapple punks
Like to spike up their hair
Peaches have fluff
All the way down their throats
Bananas are funny
Because they wear coats.

White grapes are smooth faced
Like bottles of wine
Papayas will only
Go out when it's fine
Gooseberries are shy
Some say they are wimps
Bananas are funny
In the fingers of chimps.

Bird

See the little birdie
Bouncing on its feet,
Whistling a happy tune
Tweet! Tweet! Tweet!
See the little birdie
Dropping all its poo,
Messing up my windscreen
Shoo! Shoo! Shoo!

C
c

Car

Car goes brmm brrmm
Car goes whorr whorr
Car goes phew phew
Car goes roar roar
Car goes wheeee wheee
Car goes splash splash
Car goes squeal squeal
Car goes crash crash

Car goes bang bang
Car goes blink blink
Car goes boing boing
Car goes clink clink
Car goes whish whish
Car goes pfaw pfaw
Car goes ffut ffut
Car goes no more.

Cats

Cats like roofs
Cats like sun
Cats like wool
Cats like fun.

Cats like milk
Cats like dishes
Cats like mice
Cats like fishes.

Cats like licks
Cats like hairs
Cats like laps
Cats like chairs.

Cats like rugs
Cats like mats
Cats like strokes
Cats don't like cats.

C c

Cow

'You silly cow,'
I said to the cow
And the cow said,
'I'm quite sane.'
'You daft old bat,'
I said to the bat
And the bat said,
'Feel my brain.'

'You stubborn mule,'
I said to the mule
And the mule said,
'I've got power.'
'You dirty pig,'
I said to the pig
And the pig said,
'I can't shower.'

'You scaredy cat,'
I said to the cat
And the cat said,
'I'm prepared.'
You timid mouse
I said to the mouse
And the mouse said,
'I'm not scared.'

'You vicious fox,'
I said to the fox
And the fox said,
'I'm not rough.'
'You lazy dog,'
I said to the dog
And the dog said,
'Wuff, wuff, wuff.'

D
d

Dog

There once was a dog
who went for a jog
in very thick fog.
Because of the fog
the dog on a jog
got lost in a bog.
Poor dog on a jog,
poor dog in a bog,
he sank like a log
in the fog
in the bog
and instead of a bark
there was only a glog;
a dog in a bog
going glog, glog, glog.
Poor dog in a bog
going glog,
      glog,
        g
          l
            o
              g.

Don't

Don't touch
Don't walk
Don't push
Don't talk.

Don't cry
Don't groan
Don't whinge
Don't moan.

Don't slouch
Don't slump
Don't dash
Don't jump.

Don't burp
Don't munch
Don't slurp
Don't punch.

Don't move
Don't blink
Don't smile
Don't think.

Don't sweat
Don't leave
Don't live
Don't breathe.

D
d

Drip

I want to be an ocean, blue and dark and deep
I want to be the waves that never ever sleep
I want to be the water lifting up a ship
I will be when I'm bigger but now I'm just a drip.

I want to be a geyser gushing up with force
I want to be the gurgle of a river at its source
I want to be a pool in which swimmers take a dip
I will be when I'm bigger but now I'm just a drip.

I want to be a glacier rising ghostly white
I want to be a snowstorm tumbling from a height
I want to be an ice rink where skaters slowly slip
I will be when I'm bigger but now I'm just a drip.

Ear

You can taste
without an aste.
You can see
without an ee.
You can smell
without a mell.
But without an ear
you cannot hear.

Egg

Oh lovely little eggy
I must put you in a cup
Bash you on your pointed head
And eat your insides up.
Eggy
Heggy
Bleggy
Weggy
Eat your insides up.

Elephant

Don't take your elephant
to school.
It would be cruel
to take an elephant
to school.
Elephants need grasses
not classes.
Elephants need baths
not maths.
Leave your elephant
at home.
Let it sleep.
Let it roam.
Let your ele
watch the tele.
But don't be cruel.
Don't be cruel.
Don't take your elephant
to school.

F f

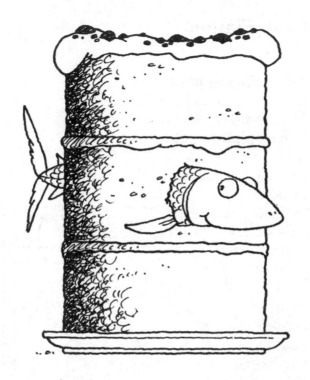

Fish

Fish cake has no
Cream or icing
It isn't served in slices.
For your party
Don't get fish cake
That's what my advice is.

Flames

Yellow ghosts walk
on invisible toes,
dance over coal
and shrink into glows.

F
f

Frog

If you want to upset a frog
don't call it Frog Face.
Call it
Human Face
Narrow Mouth
Flat Eyes
Dry Skin
Ten Toes.

Don't tell it
to hop it.
Tell it to walk.

Goose

If I met a goose
I wouldn't say BOO –
Not that I'm scared.
I've better things to do.

G
g

Grass

I am the breeze
I look for grass that bends
I am a daisy
I look for grass for friends
I am a scythe
I look for grass that mows
I am a field mouse
I look for grass that grows.

I am a cow
I look for grass to graze
I am a poet
I look for grass that sways
I am a flame
I look for grass that burns
I am a bird
I look for grass with worms.

I am a farmer
I look for grass that sells
I am a puppy
I look for grass that smells
I am a snail
I look for grass that's wet
I am a slug
I look for any grass I can get.

G
g

Gum

Chew chew chew
Chew chew chew
Gum stick
Gum stick
Gum stick
Gum.
Sticky taste
Sticky taste
Lemonade tang
Blow bubble
Blow bubble
Blow bubble BANG!

Hat

The cat should have sat
on the mat.
Instead, the cat
(that was fat)
sat on my hat.
Because the cat
that was fat
who should have sat
on the mat
instead sat on my hat,
the hat beneath the cat
became flat.
I now have a hat
which is as flat as a mat.
As a matter of fact,
it's flatter than that.
And all because
of an obstinate cat.

H h

Hippopotamus

If not in its kippo
It's having a dippo.
(The life of a hippo
Could do with more zippo.)

Holes

I like holes
in the garden
but not in my shirts
or shoes.
I like holes
in fences,
trees,
CDs,
needles,
hedgerows
and beaches
but not in lettuce leaves
or the ozone.

I i

Ink

If the world
ran out of ink
I could dr
but not drink,
I could bl
but not blink,
pigs would st
but not stink.
A strange world
don't you th?

EXAM
ROOM

CANCELLED
NO INK

Insect

An earwig
jumped off a leaf,
hit the ground
and died.
It looked like an
accidental death
but in fact was
insecticide.

OVER HERE,
SARGE!

I
i

Is

Is is a doing word
That's what the work of is is.
An is is always busy
Doing is's business.

Jack

(Best read in blues rhythm.)

Went up the hill
To try to get some drink.
Went up the hill
To try to get some drink.
I should have been more careful
But, hey, I just didn't think.

Tripped on a stone
And fell right down that hill.
Tripped on a stone
And fell right down that hill.
The pail got bent and twisted
The water, it got spilled.

I broke my head
On that tripping stone.
I broke my head
On that tripping stone.
I got to get it fixed up
Before I go back home.

J
j

Jar

Jam in the jar.
Hole in the lid.

Jar on the ledge.
Wasp in the air.

Wasp on the lid.
Wasp on the hole.

Wasp in the hole.
Wasp in the jar.

Wasp on the jam.
Jam on the wasp.

Wasp in the jam.
Jammed in the jam.

Jammed in the jar.
Jammed in the jar.

Joey*

A Joey lives in its mummy's pouch
If it should fall out, it would cry 'Ouch!'

* name given to a young kangaroo

K
k

Kite

I've got a thing
on the end of a string
that climbs higher than trees
that can ride on the breeze
like a ship on the seas.
That can dive and can glide
that can swoop and can slide
and can look down at me
as it sings
this small song:

'I've got a thing
on the end of a string
way way way down
that lives on the ground.
As I get much taller
it grows smaller and smaller
and it looks up at me
as it runs to be free.'

Knees

She thinks
she is
the bees knees.
And she almost is;

Small and hairy,
Knobbly and scary.

K k

Knickers

If I shouted SHOES!
Would that make the news?
If I shouted COAT!
Would that get your goat?
If I shouted SKIRT!
Would you get all hurt?
If I shouted SCARF!
Would that make you laugh?

If I shouted BOOT!
Would you give a hoot?
If I shouted HAT!
Would you flinch at that?
If I shouted SOCK!
Would that be a shock?
If I shouted KNICKERS!
Would you start to snicker?

Lions

(Advice to lions who wish to go to school.)

No running in hallways
No sharpening claws
No scratching on desktops
No growling or roars.

No pouncing at playtime
No mud on your feet
No killing for dinner
No playing with meat.

No chasing of chickens
No bullying beasts
No snatching from others
No mid-morning feasts.

No swishing of tails
No prowling through schools
You're welcome to join us
But these are the rules.

Loo

If you're polite
You call it 'the restroom'
If you're old
It's 'the WC'
If you're shy
You refer to 'the washroom'
If you're a dog
It's known as a tree.
If you're rude
You call it 'the bog'
If you're posh
You speak of 'the loo'
If you're out
It's 'Ladies' and 'Gents'
If you're three
It's 'potty' or 'poo'.
If you're Aussie
You call it 'the dunny'
If you're a Yank
You call it 'the head'
If you're French
Vous dissez *'la toilette'*
If you're one
You just do it in bed!

Love

The problem with writing
Poems about love
Is finding good rhymes
That aren't 'glove' or 'dove'.
There's nothing romantic
In a five-fingered glove
And no one when kissing
Can coo like a dove.
So what can be done
When push comes to shove?
Just write what you feel.
Then add stars above.

M m

Mat

The cat sat on the mat.
Why did it do that?
Was it thinking at the time
'Me and this make a rhyme'?

If so, why don't grizzly bears
Hide in stuffed armchairs?
And why don't country foxes
Nest in cardboard boxes?

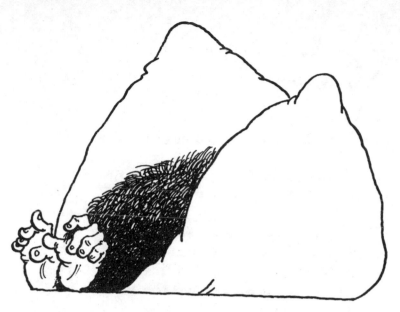

And why don't crocodiles
Slide on bathroom tiles?
And why don't alligators
Warm on radiators?

And why don't gorillas
Rest on feather pillows?
And why don't kangaroos
Bounce on comfy loos?

The mat lay under the cat.
Why did it do that?
Did it think at the time
'Me and this make a rhyme'?

M
m

Match

Out of the wood comes the stick
Out of the stick comes the match
Out of the match comes the fire
Out of the fire comes the ash

Out of the ash comes the dust
Out of the dust comes the dirt
Out of the dirt comes the seed
Out of the seed comes the shoot.

Out of the shoot comes the tree
Out of the tree comes the wood
Out of the wood comes the stick
Out of the stick comes the match

Out of the match comes the fire
Out of the match comes the fire.

Mess

You like it tidy
You like it clean
I leave a mess
To show where I've been.

Stains on the carpet
Streaks on the wall
Ink on the sofa
Mud in the hall.

Bags on the table
Boots on the chairs
Coats on the door knobs
Jeans on the stairs.

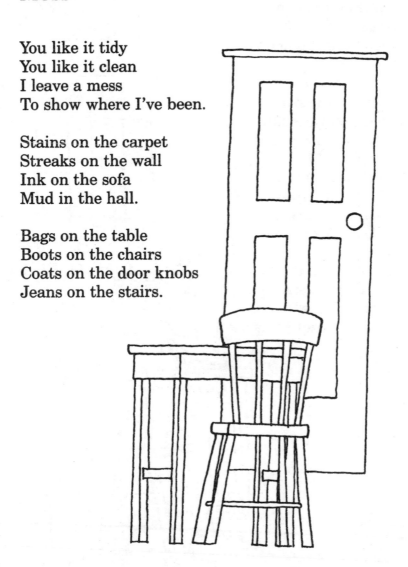

M
m

Scum in the bathtub
Paste on the door
Suds on the mirror
Floods on the floor.

Plates on the pillow
Cups on the seats
Beans on the ceiling
Crumbs on the sheets.

You like it perfect
You like it spruce.
I like it messed up
I like it loose.

You like it tidy
You like it clean
I leave a mess
To show where I've been.

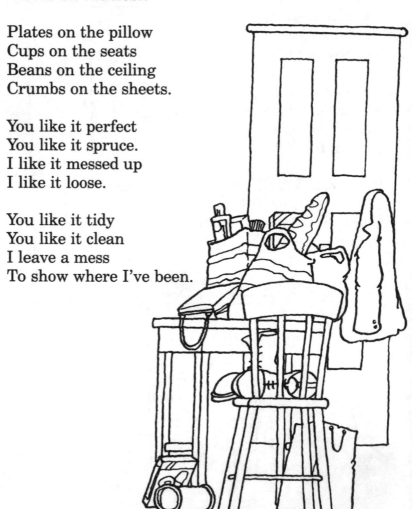

Nail

A nail
without a hammer
might as well
be dead.
A nail
needs a hammer
to hit it
on the head.

News

HILL CLIMBING COUPLE TAKE TUMBLE:
JACK CRACKS HEAD.
WALL FALL DISASTER OF EGG MAN:
DUMPTY FOUND DEAD.

TUFFET GIRL'S CREEPY SENSATION:
LARGE SPIDER SCARES.
HUGE WOOL BONANZA OF BLACK SHEEP:
SHARP RISE IN SHARES.

DEATH PLUNGE OF NEW TREETOP BABY:
CRADLE IN FALL.
ROBIN DEATH SPARROW SUSPICION:
FLY REVEALS ALL.

SPACE COW IN BLAST-OFF FOR MOON RIDE:
DOG LAUGH RINGS.
DISH AND SPOON FLEE IN LOVE TANGLE:
CAT PLAYS STRINGS

Night

Dusk, they say, gathers
but when was it spread?
Stars, they say, peep out
but which has a head?
The moon, they say, rises
but how can it stand?
The night, they say, falls
but where does it land?

O
o

Oil

Cars and trucks are made for it
Billions are paid for it.
Oil. We need that stuff.

Tars and plastics come from it
Central heating runs on it.
Oil. We need that stuff.

Cyclists grease their wheels with it
Countries do their deals with it.
Oil. We need that stuff.

The Middle East has lots of it
John Paul Getty made pots from it.
Oil. We need that stuff.

Companies still bore for it
Armies go to war for it.
Oil. We need that stuff.

Life is underpinned by it
The ozone layer's thinned by it.
Oil. We need that stuff.

Disposable cups and nylon tights
Diesel trains and long-haul flights
Lipstick, glue, PVC
We need that stuff.

Oil in a barrel
Oil in a can
Oil in a pipeline
Oil in the sand.

Well, we need that stuff
We need that stuff.
There's not much left
But we need that stuff.

(Modelled on Adrian Mitchell's
poem 'Stufferation'.)

Onion

Like you I make
   eyes water
Like you I
   sometimes sting.
Like you I'm
   many layered
Like you my skin
   is thin.

Orange

They say there's no rhyme for an orange
Except in a language that's forange
The peach has a beach
And the lime has a chime
But the orange has nothing. How storange.

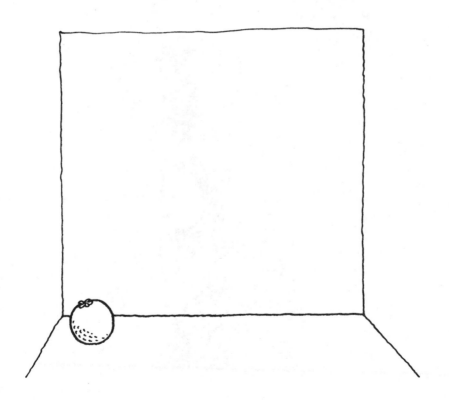

P
p

P

P in philosophy
P in prayer
P in parachute
P in pear.

P in porcelain
P in plants
P in privacy
P in pants.

Prayers

Do my prayers go up
through the ceiling,
do they fly in the atmosphere?
If I whisper
or talk in my head,
do you think that God can still hear?

Do my words arrive
with my name on
or do I need to add an address?
If I fall asleep
while I'm speaking,
does God think my dreams are requests?

If I say a prayer
every evening,
will all of my wishes come true?
Do you think that God
prays to his children,
and hopes that they answer him too?

P p

Punch

Hi! My name's Judy.
I've met this fantastic new guy
Down at the beach.
It was like, BOOM! I don't know why.

He had me falling about.
He was cracking these awful jokes
And he wouldn't stop.
He seems so different. Not like most blokes.

He says he'll call me.
We're getting together for lunch
in a day or two.
He carries a stick. Says his name's Punch.

Q
q

Queen

I have a cap
You have a crown
I have a coat
You have a gown
I have a badge
You have a brooch
I have a bike
You have a coach.

I have a house
You have a hall
I have a dance
You have a ball
I have a coin
You have a hoard
I have a stick
You have sword.

I have a ring
You have a stone
I have a chair
You have a throne
I have a drum
You have a band
I have a lawn
You have a land.

Questions

Miss, you ask me questions
But I refuse to crack.
I was always taught that
It's rude to answer back.

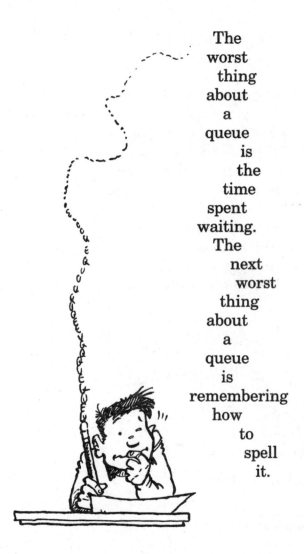

Queue

The
worst
thing
about
a
queue
is
the
time
spent
waiting.
The
next
worst
thing
about
a
queue
is
remembering
how
to
spell
it.

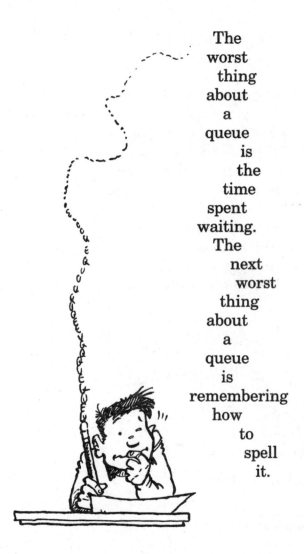

R
r

Rain

I feed your plants
I put out flames
And all you do
Is call me names:

Bad rain, nasty rain,
Terrible rain, awful rain
Foul rain, wretched rain,
Horrible rain, evil rain.

I quench your thirst
I fill your sea
And this is what
You think of me:

Bad rain, nasty rain,
Terrible rain, awful rain,
Foul rain, wretched rain,
Horrible rain, evil rain.

I wash your streets
I give you drink
I should be praised
Don't you think?

Good rain, gentle rain,
Clean rain, precious rain,
Kind rain, careful rain,
Saving rain, lovely rain.

Red

Red is the colour
Of my true love's lips
Red is the colour
Of the evening sky
Red is the colour
Of a robin's breast
Red is the colour
Of a bloodshot eye.

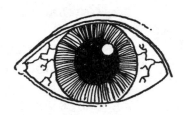

Red is the colour
Of a furnace flame
Red is the colour
Of a rambling rose
Red is the colour
Of the setting sun
Red is the colour
Of a boxer's nose.

Red is the colour
Of a Martian day
Red is the colour
Of a bleeding gum
Red is the colour
Of a Man U shirt
Red is the colour
Of a baboon's bum.

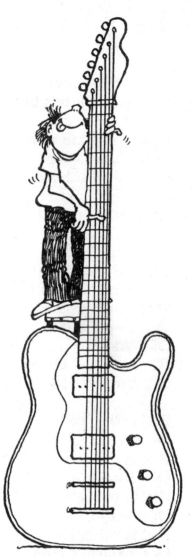

Rhubarb

Rhubarb rhubarb
Rhubarb a doo barb
Rhubarb a doo barb
A bop bamboo.

Roo roo roo
Roo roo roo
Roo tooti too
On the top bamboo.

Bar bar bar
Bar bar bar
Bar bar Barbara Ann
On the blip blam blam.

Rhubarb rhubarb
What you gonna do barb
On the blip blam blam
Of the top bamboo?
Rhubarb boo barb
What you gonna do barb
On the blip blam blam
Of the bop bamboo?

It's rhubarb rhubarb
What you gonna chew barb
Stew barb, stew barb,
Who barb? You barb.
Rhubarb rhubarb
on a rap blam boom!

S

Many of our words
Begin with an S.
E.g. suspicious,
Survivor, success.

I could have said stink
(In fact, I just did)
Shuffle or shadow
Sam, Sara or Sid.

Many more of our words
Don't begin with an S.
Examples? Never,
No, maybe and yes.

Therefore, to sum up,
To tell you what's what:
Some words are S words
And some words are not.

Sausages

If you're in a paddywack
If your mood is strange
Just say the word SAUSAGES
And things will start to change.

You can't be broken-hearted
Or wear a look of gloom
When a noun like SAUSAGES
Resounds around a room.

The cat has just gone missing.
Your pet fly has just died.
Count to ten. Shout SAUSAGES.
You'll see the funny side.

Your team has just been beaten
The top's gone from your pen
You need a sound like SAUSAGES
To lift you up again.

So when you have a problem,
No matter what it is,
You'll always feel much better
If you call out SAUSAGES.

Socks

Socks don't seem to like my feet
They just don't want to stay.
Every time that two get washed
There's one that runs away.

Tiger

Tiger! Tiger! burning bright
Who was it set your fur alight?
Wait right there. Don't run away.
I'll call the RSPCA.

(The first line refers to William Blake's famous
poem 'The Tyger'.)

T
t

Titanic

The old wreck wakes up
In its ocean bed
Straightens its back
And raises its head.

The flags give a wave
And funnels un-bend
The rust turns to steel
The snapped cables mend.

Bones re-meet sockets
And slowly slide in
The skulls of the dead
Retrieve all their skin.

Engines are turning
The anchor is raised
The portholes are shut
The furnaces blaze.

A sucking of brine
A swirling of sand
A hymn is picked up
On brass by a band.

The big ship floats up –
A shape made of black –
And breaks into light.
Titanic is back!

Train

Chicketty chack
Chicketty chack
The railway train
Runs down the track.

Chicketty choo
Chicketty choo
The 10:05
Is passing through.

Chicketty chong
Chicketty chong
We're gaining speed
It won't be long.

Chicketty cheer
Chicketty cheer
We're slowing down
We must be near.

Chicketty cho
Chicketty cho
The train has stopped
It's time to go.

U u

Umbrella

Umber the rella
it's safe from storms,
umber the rella
it's dry.
Umber the rella
I hear the sound
of rain falling down
from the sky.

Umber the rella
I find some shade,
umber the rella
it's cool.
Umber the rella
I see the sun
dance on the waves
of the pool.

Umber the rella
a gale gets up,
umber the rella
it blows.
Umber the rella
the wind is strong
and up in the air
it goes.

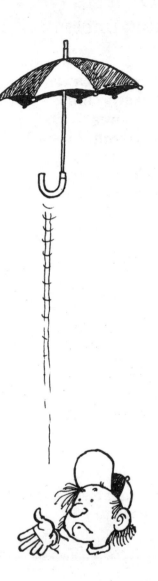

Uncle

My Uncle
Jim
was
slim.
That's all
I recall
about
him.

U u

Up

'What's up?'
She asked.

'The sky,'
Said I.

'The price
Of ice cream.
Pigeons.
Crime.
Balloons.
The moon.

'That's
what's up,'
I said.
'That's
what's up.'

Vampire

As a vampire, Victor
Was a bit of a dud.
He liked having sharp teeth
But he couldn't stand blood.

'You've got to drink up son,'
Said his father one night.
'You won't grow up strong
If you're frightened to bite.'

So out Victor ventured
On the lookout for skin
And found something smooth
To sink his fangs in.

Victor snapped and he snapped
Like a wolf on the loose
And his mouth filled with bits
While his chin ran with juice.

'I've done it dear father,'
Shouted Victor with pride.
'I'm a vampire tonight!
My victim has died.'

A vampire he was, but
Not such a scary 'un.
He'd bitten a tomato
So remained, vegetarian.

V
v

Vandal

Oh what are you doing
You vandal alone
With your aerosol can
Your stick and your stone?

I do something secret
I do it at night
I do it in letters
That stand big and bright.

Oh where are you going
You vandal alone
With your aerosol can
Your stick and your stone?

I go to the rail track
I go to the mall
I go to the car park
And spray on the wall.

Oh why do you do it
You vandal alone
With your aerosol can
Your stick and your stone?

I do it for pleasure
I do it for fame
I do it for danger
And for my own name.

Vicars

Your vicar can score
My vicar is quicker
Your vicar can swerve
My vicar's much slicker.

Your vicar can tap
My vicar's a flicker
Your vicar can pass
My vicar's a kicker.

Your vicar gives up
My vicar's a sticker
Your vicar just lost
My vicar's a victor.

Wiggle

A wiggle's when you
squirm.
No, that's a wriggle.
A wiggle's when you
smirk.
No, that's a giggle.

A wiggle's when you
scrawl.
No, that's a squiggle.

A wiggle's when you jerk.
Yes, that's a wiggle.

A wiggle's when you jerk.
That's a wiggle.

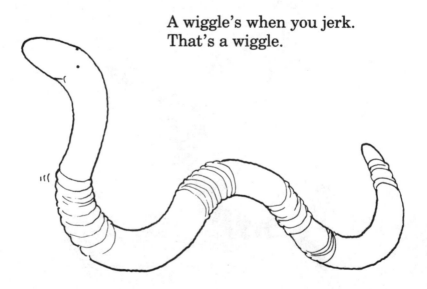

Wind

I am the north wind
I like to blow
I am the south wind
I like to bring snow.

I am the west wind
I like to thrill
I am the east wind
I like to chill.

I am the no wind
I like to soothe
I am the stillness
With me nothing moves.

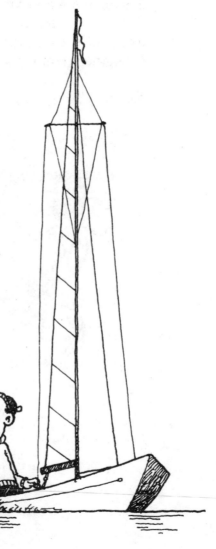

W
w

World

The world's a balloon
With dirt stuck on top.
Be careful when digging
In case it goes POP!

X

X is a kiss
X is a site
X is the mark
For something not right.

X is a ray
X is forbidden
X is the spot
Where treasure is hidden.

X is a sign
X is a trail
X is the cross
With thorns and with nails.

X is exclusive
X is exciting
X always looks
Extremely inviting.

X
x

Xmas

I wanted Christmas tree fairies
You gave me an angel instead.
I wanted Rudolph the Reindeer
You gave me cows in a shed.

I wanted cards in the mailbox
You gave me words for the poor
I wanted a sleigh ride with Santa
You gave me a bed in the straw.

I wanted gifts wrapped in paper
You gave me news of a birth
I wanted a happy new year
You gave me peace upon earth.

Xylophone

I was given one for Christmas
I played it once or twice
I managed 'Baa Baa Black Sheep'
And (almost) 'Three Blind Mice'.

Before Boxing Day was done
I'd put it in its box.
The coloured bars got loosened
The music book got lost.

A xylophone's not trendy
Like keyboards or guitar.
I've never ever heard of
A xylophonic star.

The only thing it's good for
(I say this with regret)
Is filling up the X page
In a children's alphabet.

Y
y

Yap

(A limerick for dogs)

Yap yap yap yap yap yap park park
Yap yap yap yap yap yap dark dark
Yap yap yap yap prowl
Yap yap yap yap growl
Yap yap yap yap yap yap bark bark.

Yo-yo

My life as a yo-yo?
A bit all over the place
A bit to and fro
A bit of a spin
A bit stop and go.

A bit of a stretch
A bit tightly wound
A bit of a bind
A bit up and down.

A bit knotted up
A bit slow and slack
A bit of a tumble.
But,

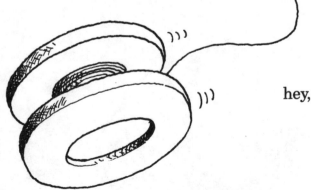

hey,

I bounce back.

Y
y

Yuk

Appetisers
Cocktail of slug juice
Sliced worm brunch
Dog's breath dorritos
Snail shell crunch.

Main course
Shark's eye with dandruff
Pulverised rat
Mouse tails in snake slime
Fried wing of bat.

Dessert
The stuff that spurts from
A squashed dead fly
Custard with cat's hair
Toe jam pie.

Z

'Four hundred years ago the Z was so worthless
it was used as a term of insult.'
                    The Times, 1 October 2005

We don't like you, Z.
You're out of your head.
You're too screwed up,
too squashed. Get lost.

You look like a snake;
a crushed can; a crack;
something about to break.

You're not like me, says G.
You've got no curls, says C.
Where's your belly? says B.
Where's your hat? says T.

Words don't want to
begin with you.
There's too much hiss,
too much bend.
You can stay
in the alphabet, Z,
but, get to the end.

Zebra

The lion crossing is golden
The leopard crossing has spots
The elephant crossing is grey
And of it there's lots and lots.

The rhino crossing has horns on
The hedgehog crossing can prick
The monkey crossing is furry
But also incredibly quick.

The flamingo crossing has pinks in
The peacock crossing has blues
The zebra crossing has blacks and whites
And that's the one that I use.

Zoo

Deep down in the forest
I came to a zoo
And inside the cages
Were people like you.

And watching the cages
Were animal crowds
Who pointed at people
And sniggered out loud

At the way that they talked
The clothes that they wore
The two feet they walked on
And what they were for.

'They can't swing from treetops,'
A monkey complained.
'Their faces are ugly,'
A young hippo claimed.

'Their necks are like tree stumps,'
Said Mrs Giraffe.
'And where are their stripes?'
Said Zebra, and laughed.

'Their fur has gone missing,'
A chimpanzee shared.
'They've too many legs,'
A python declared.

'They need their teeth sharpened,'
Was Tiger's report.
'And weight on their bellies,'
An elephant thought.

Deep down in the forest
I came to a zoo
And inside the cages
Were people like you.

Also by Steve Turner

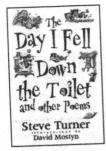

A roller-coaster ride from the crazy corners of dreams to the big questions of life – and one or two bathroom mishaps! Over 120,000 copies sold!

Welcome to a world of embarrassing dads and smelly feet in this quirky look at the pressures and pains of growing up...

Who's stuck in the bathroom? Do televisions watch too many people? Do I talk in my sleep? A hilarious romp through the day from midnight to midnight.

We all ask big questions about ourselves, other people and the world we live in. Here are some humorous and thought-provoking poetic answers.

Reviews

'If you like your poetry to make you laugh, Steve Turner's your man.'
The Daily Telegraph

'Highly observant, often poignant... but always fresh and funny.'
Nick Park, creator of Wallace and Gromit

'Wry, witty and wise – Steve Turner is the young person's poet laureate.'
Frank Barrett, The Mail on Sunday

'One of the most original and child-friendly voices to emerge in the last few years.'
The Sunday Telegraph